www.FrantoniaPollins.com

One Powerful Question

FRANTONIA POLLINS

ONE POWERFUL QUESTION

40 Days & 40 Nights: A Guided Journey of Intentional Self Discovery

Published by
Frantonia Pollins Media International
Copyright © 2011 by Frantonia Pollins

Unless otherwise indicated, all scripture taken from The King James Version of the Bible "

Printed in United Stated of America

ISBN-13: 978-0615435336

Dedication

This book is lovingly dedicated to each and every one of the Sacred Spirits who agreed to act as guides along my journey to Self.

A very special thanks to my beautiful daughter, Scheherazade for choosing to enter this experience through me. You alone have taught me more & shown me more than one could ever hope for in a million lifetimes.
I LOVE YOU to the moon and back again!

And last but not least, a "cyber" thank you to all of my Facebook friends; for the inspiration and encouragement to pursue this dream.

One Powerful Question

Introduction

The *"One Powerful Question"* Book Series was organically born out of my daily practice of connecting with Source - through meditation and journaling.

By allowing the Divine to flow through and speak to me, I found myself both asking and being asked some of the most profound, thought-provoking and world changing questions ever!

As a means of inspiring the masses, I was led to share these thoughts on one of the most popular social media networks of our day. I could never have imagined the response I would receive - hundreds of daily requests asking that I compile these powerful questions into a book. And now **here it is!**

The purpose of this book is to provide you with an easy-to-read collection of thought provoking questions & ideas intended to be the "compass" along your journey to discovering the deepest Truths hidden within your thoughts, feelings, attitudes & answers.

Your 40 Day / 40 Night journey requires a commitment of 15 minutes each morning and 15 minutes each evening. You are certainly entitled to make a larger investment of time; however, in order to reap the full benefit, less time would not be advised. My suggestion is that you place this book along with an ink pen or pencil on the night stand next to your bed; this enables you to make these exercises the VERY FIRST thing you do each morning when you awaken and the FINAL thing you do each evening before retiring.

THE MORNING EXERCISE:

Upon awakening each morning take notice of all that you have to be grateful for; and give thanks.

Give thanks as you breathe deeply and notice the effortless performance of your respiratory system.

Give thanks for the rhythmic heartbeat which requires not even the slightest command from you.

Give thanks for the life sustaining blood flowing through each vein as the carrier of nutrients to each and every organ; the carrier of oxygen to your brain.

Give thanks for cognition and ability to not only imagine a thing but the will to manifest that thing into your very own reality.

Give thanks to your creator for the gift of a brand new day filled with new opportunities to make deeper discoveries about your Self.

Take another deep breathe and simply **Give thanks!!**

You are now ready to begin YOUR journey.

Each day begins with a "Divine Commentary," within which lies a powerful and evocative question designed to prompt a deeper realization of Self.

After reading the "Divine Commentary", take a few minutes to silently reflect on what you have read. Fully and deeply allow yourself to ponder the question. Pay close attention to how the commentary and the question make you feel. Take note of what feels comfortable to you; in your heart, your soul and your Spirit. Notice what makes you feel uncomfortable, resistant and challenges your current stance.

After silently reflecting on the "Divine Commentary" you will find the "Powerful Statement of Intention". This **Principle** affirmation is offered as an integral part of the road map along your journey. This affirmation sets the tone or intention for what you plan to experience throughout each day. In other words, it is the compass which sets the mental direction and ultimately determines the final destination on your journey to Self.

Each day you are to read the "Powerful Statement of Intention" **aloud**, rather than silently to yourself, **no less than three times.** Why aloud? **YOUR** words are the Powerful wings on which your intentions fly.

The most widely known account of the process of creation began with the Most High **BOLDLY SPEAKING** its True intentions; commanding the Universe to begin. There is no greater motivation than hearing the vibrational frequency of your own voice speak empowering & affirmative words which   resonate with the deepest part of your soul to bring about that which you truly desire.

Now that you have conditioned your Mind to receive and reflect the Truth, recall the thoughts and feelings you experienced while reflecting on the "Divine Commentary". Use the journal page to set the intention to discover more about yourself as it relates to the One Powerful Question posed in the "Divine Commentary".

Set the intention for your desired outcome for today. Set the intention to observe what changes or adjustments you must make in order to bring about that outcome today. Set the intention to pay closer attention to your feelings as it relates to the One Powerful Question today? Set the intention to release ALL longstanding judgments which hinder the deeper knowledge of Self today.

This exercise will help you to INTENTIONALLY focus your energy for the day. You are now mentally, Spiritually, emotionally AND intentionally ready to begin your day.

THE EVENING EXERCISE:

Before retiring to sleep for the evening, read and   receive the Spirit of the message found in "Tonight's Classic Inspiration". These thoughts, quotes & expressions where Intentionally selected to show you the timeless and ABSOLUTE nature of Truth.

Mentally   review your day by reflecting on the ways in which you were able to apply and express the principles found in both the   modern day "Divine Commentary" and the "Classic Inspiration".

You are now ready for the evening journal. Begin by reading "Tonight's Affirmative Statement of TRUTH" aloud. Allow yourself to accept and absorb that these words are true for you.

In the journal space provided, feel free to write your feelings, thoughts, ideas and experiences as it relates to the intentions you set for the day. Through this writing process, you are able to discover things about yourself that you may never have considered.

Once you have completed the Evening Journal, once again **give thanks** to the Most High. Now you are free to begin tomorrow with a new awareness of Self.

Throughout this 40 Day / 40 Night process, you can expect to see great changes in your life as you integrate this daily practice in an intentional effort to know your Self more deeply. There will be days when this process will allow you to easily embrace new and deeper discoveries about your Self. However, there will also be days when the questions and affirmations might present unforeseen challenges or resistance as the light is shined on the often dark and undiscovered parts of your Self. I will simply encourage you to be patient as you TRUST the process and KNOW that ALL is in Divine Order.

Enjoy this journey!!

WHOSE THOUGHTS ARE THOSE YOU'RE THINKING?

Why do we allow the mass media to
constantly bombard us with reports
of recession, murder, sickness,
world-wide injustice and
financial doom & gloom?

So much exposure to negative news
can begin to take it's toll on
the human psyche.

On those days when you begin
to feel that you just can not go on,
TURN OFF THE TV!
UNPLUG THE PHONE
& go into the silence!

In this Sacred Silence, take note that the
temporary "appearance" of negativity
and defeat is only an illusion!!

ONLY through clarity of Mind,
Shall the Truth be revealed.

Today's Powerful Statement of INTENTION

KNOWING that I AM blessed with the Sacred gift of Divine awareness, Today and everyday I INTENTIONALLY choose only those thoughts, actions & beliefs which shape, influence & support the powerful purpose for my life which is revealed to me everyday by The Most High.

My chief Intention for today is:

_____

_____

_____

_____

_____

_____

_____

_____

_____

_____

_____

_____

Tonight's Classic Inspiration

*For I reckon
that these
present sufferings
are not worthy
to be compared
with the glory
which shall be
revealed
in us.*
- Romans 8:18

One Powerful Question

Tonight's Affirmative Statement of TRUTH

I set the intention to clear away the mental distractions of the world by entering into the Sacred Silence of my daily meditation

Today's Divine Commentary

HOW MANY OF YOUR DREAMS HAVE YOU ALLOWED TO DIE?

What part of the passionate
life that you have imagined
for yourself needs
to be "resurrected?"

Boldly SPEAK life into the dreams
that you have allowed be buried
in the barren desert of
doubt, fear, insecurity
and Self-betrayal.

Declare that today is the day
that you will bring your dreams
back to life so that your Divine gifts
can be of service to the world.

KNOWING that I AM blessed with the Sacred gift of Divine awareness, Today and everyday I INTENTIONALLY choose only those thoughts, actions & beliefs which shape, influence & support the powerful purpose for my life which is revealed to me everyday by The Most High.

My chief Intention for today is:

*Again he said
unto me,
Prophesy
upon these bones,
and say unto them,
O ye dry bones,
hear the word
of the LORD.
Thus saith the Lord
GOD unto these bones;
Behold,
I will cause breath
to enter into you,
and ye shall live*
-Ezekiel 37:4-5

Tonight's Affirmative Statement of TRUTH

Today I BOLDY speak life into my dreams and with unwavering faith, I eagerly seize the Divine opportunities that continuously come my way.

Today's Divine Commentary

HOW MUCH LOVE CAN YOU SHARE WITH THE WORLD TODAY?

The belief that we are separate
from each other and therefore different
creates great conflict and a lack
of the Agape or unconditional
love that is required to heal the world.

When we re-cognize that there is but
One Source from which we all come,
we will begin to express Supreme love
for and to ALL of mankind.

Be consciously aware of your thoughts,
attitudes and actions toward
EVERYONE whose path you are
blessed to cross today.

Make it your business to
"LOVE ON THEM;"
for we are all connected and
what affects one,
affects us all.

Today's Powerful Statement of INTENTION

KNOWING that I AM blessed with the Sacred gift of Divine awareness, Today and everyday I INTENTIONALLY choose only those thoughts, actions & beliefs which shape, influence & support the powerful purpose for my life which is revealed to me everyday by The Most High.

My chief Intention for today is:

Tonight's Classic Inspiration

*Forget not
to show love
unto strangers:
for thereby some
have entertained
angels
unawares*
-Hebrews 13:2

Tonight's Affirmative Statement of TRUTH

*I AM an expression of the One Power,
One Source, One Love from which all things
come and I share this endless supply of
Divine love with all.*

Today's Divine Commentary

CAN YOU SPEAK PEACE TO THE STORMS IN YOUR LIFE?

Whatever the storms are in your life;
whether it's a financial storm,
an emotional storm,
the storm of loneliness,
abandonment or isolation:

KNOW that the power to "calm"
the storms of life
FIRST begins with calling forth
the God that dwells within
to remind you that the
power of life AND death
lies in your own tongue.

You must believe that Divine order,
love, peace & prosperity
are your GOD-INTENDED
birth-right.

Speak truth to power and
COMMAND
the storms in your life
to CEASE!

Today's Powerful Statement of INTENTION

KNOWING that I AM blessed with the Sacred gift of Divine awareness, Today and everyday I INTENTIONALLY choose only those thoughts, actions & beliefs which shape, influence & support the powerful purpose for my life which is revealed to me everyday by The Most High.

My chief Intention for today is:

Tonight's Classic Inspiration

*And he awoke,
and rebuked
the wind,
and said
unto the sea,
Peace,
be still.
And the wind
ceased,
and there was a
great calm*
-Mark 4:39

Tonight's Affirmative Statement of TRUTH

Today and everyday I call on the indwelling Power of God to speak peace to the storms. I use my words to command the life that I desire to come forth .

CAN YOU STAND ALONE IN ORDER TO STAND WITH GOD?

When we experience major changes
such as divorce, job loss
or even death,
we often feel as though
God has left us alone.

Only in the silent solitude and
stillness of the womb does the
growth and preparation
for the birthing of
Infinite Possibilities
take place.

The very thing that "appears" to be
an upheaval or an over-turning of
our "normal" life, is simply
the preparation necessary
for The Most High to bring forth
THROUGH you, TO the world,
the service, purpose and mission
for which you were intended.

KNOWING that I AM blessed with the Sacred gift of Divine awareness, Today and everyday I INTENTIONALLY choose only those thoughts, actions & beliefs which shape, influence & support the powerful purpose for my life which is revealed to me everyday by The Most High.

My chief Intention for today is:

*Before
I formed thee
in the belly
I knew thee,
and before thou
camest forth
out of the womb
I sanctified thee;*
-Jeremiah 1:5

Tonight's Affirmative Statement of TRUTH

I remain open & receptive to the growth which
will bring forth my God-given gifts & talents
for I know that I AM being prepared
for a Divine and mighty work.

Today's Divine Commentary

WHAT KIND OF ENERGY HAVE YOU INVITED INTO YOUR LIFE?

The Law of Vibrational Alignment
(aka The Law of Attraction) simply means: That
which I AM seeking - pursuing,
worrying or fretting over, giving thought
or attention to or allowing myself to be aroused/
moved by, is also seeking me.

The "attractive energy" of the thoughts
that each of us carries in our minds
is extremely powerful.

Everything and everyone that we allow to
enter our "data-sphere" carries with them
and exchanges with us an energy
which either drains or empowers us.

Be careful to what and to WHOM you
attach and exchange your mental,
spiritual, emotional AND sexual energy.

Today's Powerful Statement of INTENTION

KNOWING that I AM blessed with the Sacred gift of Divine awareness, Today and everyday I INTENTIONALLY choose only those thoughts, actions & beliefs which shape, influence & support the powerful purpose for my life which is revealed to me everyday by The Most High.

My chief Intention for today is:

_____

_____

_____

_____

_____

_____

_____

_____

_____

_____

_____

*No temptation
can gravitate to a man
unless there is that
in his heart which is
capable of
responding to it*

-James Allen

Tonight's Affirmative Statement of TRUTH

I AM connected to the One Infinite Mind wherein all of my desires have already been perfectly and completely met.

Today's Divine Commentary

ARE YOU BOLD ENOUGH TO AGREE WITH GOD ABOUT YOUR DESTINY?

Take note that whenever a Divine idea
is presented to you, it is the
Genesis of the work for which
The Most High has purposefully,
specifically and intentionally
created YOU.

Long before you were even aware of
your own existence,
you were FULLY EQUIPPED by
the Great One;
as the intention was set for you to
manifest & co-create
magnificence.

BE BOLD in your endeavors
and KNOW that YOU were
CHOSEN, DESTINED
for such a time as this.

Today's Powerful Statement of INTENTION

KNOWING that I AM blessed with the Sacred gift of Divine awareness, Today and everyday I INTENTIONALLY choose only those thoughts, actions & beliefs which shape, influence & support the powerful purpose for my life which is revealed to me everyday by The Most High.

My chief Intention for today is:

_____

_____

_____

_____

_____

_____

_____

_____

_____

_____

_____

_____

Tonight's Classic Inspiration

*We are
but as the
instrument of
Heaven.
Our work
is not design,
but destiny.*
-Owen Meredith

Tonight's Affirmative Statement of TRUTH

*I agree with God that I AM fully equipped And
Divinely destined to manifest success in
my life today and every day.*

Today's Divine Commentary

ARE YOU WILLING TO ALLOW YOUR PAIN TO PERFECT YOU?

Whenever you feel like giving up,
find inspiration in the persistence and
FAITH of J.K. Rowlings -
Author of the Harry Potter book series.

In the midst of grief, love-lost to a
broken marriage, sudden single
Mother hood, dependence on public
assistance & welfare and a diagnosis of
severe clinical depression,
she chose to hold on to
the slightest thread of FAITH
in order to heed the call of her SOUL.

She is now one of the wealthiest
most renowned authors in the world.

HOLD ON TO YOUR FAITH
AND DON'T EVER GIVE UP
ON YOUR DREAMS!!!

Today's Powerful Statement of INTENTION

KNOWING that I AM blessed with the Sacred gift of Divine awareness, Today and everyday I INTENTIONALLY choose only those thoughts, actions & beliefs which shape, influence & support the powerful purpose for my life which is revealed to me everyday by The Most High.

My chief Intention for today is:

Tonight's Classic Inspiration

*What does not
destroy me,
makes me
strong*
-Friedrich Nietzsche

Tonight's Affirmative Statement of TRUTH

Even in the face of uncertainty, I seek the inspiration to Faithfully KNOW that I AM being prepared for a mighty work.

Today's Divine Commentary

ARE YOU LIVING UP TO YOUR SPIRITUAL RESPONSIBILITIES?

In the Book of Genesis,
to every living thing was given
the commandment to
"Be fruitful AND multiply!"
This means that we all have a
Spiritual responsibility to
sow the seeds required to
manifest or bring forth
a bountiful harvest.

Each and every day,
the Most High gifts us with
seeds filled with the potential to bear
a garden filled with
Infinite possibilities.

The only way to increase your harvest
is to plant your seeds wisely by
aligning your FAITH with
the corresponding actions
necessary to turn
"possibilities" into "PROBABILITIES"

Today's Powerful Statement of INTENTION

KNOWING that I AM blessed with the Sacred gift of Divine awareness, Today and everyday I INTENTIONALLY choose only those thoughts, actions & beliefs which shape, influence & support the powerful purpose for my life which is revealed to me everyday by The Most High.

My chief Intention for today is:

_____

_____

_____

_____

_____

_____

_____

_____

_____

_____

_____

Tonight's Classic Inspiration

His lord said unto him,
Well done, thou good
and faithful servant:
thou hast been
faithful over
a few things,
I will make thee
ruler over many
- Matt 25:21

Tonight's Affirmative Statement of TRUTH

I now accept responsibility for wisely aligning my actions with the faith necessary to bring about my desired harvest.

Today's Divine Commentary

WHEN GOD CHOOSES YOU, WHO ARE YOU TO SAY NO?

Too often the ego or the less evolved
parts of ourselves will
attempt to resist
the "call" that is made
to the Spirit during those
moments of Divine inspiration.

The ideas that have been
dropped down into your Spirit
do not belong to you.

You have been Intentionally chosen by
the Most High as a fully equipped
Holy incubator THROUGH which
Sacred work will be born.

Although the birthing of
these Divine ideas may appear
to require painful labor,
this is not the time to abort
God's vision for your life!

Today's Powerful Statement of INTENTION

**KNOWING that I AM blessed with the Sacred gift
of Divine awareness, Today and everyday I
INTENTIONALLY choose only those thoughts,
actions & beliefs which shape, influence & support
the powerful purpose for my life which is revealed
to me everyday by The Most High.**

My chief Intention for today is:

_____

_____

_____

_____

_____

_____

_____

_____

_____

_____

_____

To tend,
unfailingly,
unflinchingly,
towards
a goal,
is the
secret of
success
-Anna Pavlova

Tonight's Affirmative Statement of TRUTH

I release all resistance to my "calling." I FULLY
surrender by joyously saying "Yes!"
to my Divine assignment.

Today's Divine Commentary

WHAT CHANGE WILL YOU BRING TO THE WORLD?

When we take time to reflect
on the lives and legacies of
the well known talents, celebrities,
healers and world changers who
have recently made their transitions;
we tend to separate ourselves
from them thinking that they
possessed "something"
that we do not.

We must know that we ALL
come here with a Spiritual
assignment which no one else
on this planet can do
the way that we can.

YOU ARE HERE TO CHANGE THE WORLD!

Make sure to LIVE YOUR LIFE FULL OUT!
So that when you transition, the world
will know that you were here and that a
difference was made because
you touched the lives of so many.

Today's Powerful Statement of INTENTION

KNOWING that I AM blessed with the Sacred gift of Divine awareness, Today and everyday I INTENTIONALLY choose only those thoughts, actions & beliefs which shape, influence & support the powerful purpose for my life which is revealed to me everyday by The Most High.

My chief Intention for today is:

_____

_____

_____

_____

_____

_____

_____

_____

_____

_____

Everyone has his own specific vocation or mission in life; everyone must carry out a concrete assignment that demands fulfillment

-Viktor Frankl

Tonight's Affirmative Statement of TRUTH

Today I choose to live my life to the fullest.
I AM here as a Sacred vessel
to change the world!

Today's Divine Commentary

ARE YOU READY TO DECLARE YOUR DIVINE INDEPENDENCE?

Are you REALLY Free?

The dictionary defines independence as freedom from the control, influence, support or aid of others.

In order to truly reveal
the Divinity that desires to be
expressed through your life,
you must first MANIFEST your
independence and then
DECLARE it to the world.

Once you are FREE,
CHOOSE to embrace ONLY
those things that super-naturally
propel your Spirit
toward the evolutionary shift
that is NOW happening
in the Universe.

Today's Powerful Statement of INTENTION

KNOWING that I AM blessed with the Sacred gift of Divine awareness, Today and everyday I INTENTIONALLY choose only those thoughts, actions & beliefs which shape, influence & support the powerful purpose for my life which is revealed to me everyday by The Most High.

My chief Intention for today is:

_____

_____

_____

_____

_____

_____

_____

_____

_____

_____

_____

Tonight's Classic Inspiration

*I prefer to
be true to myself,
even at the hazard
of incurring the ridicule
of others,
rather than to
be false,
and to incur
my own abhorrence*
- Frederick Douglass

One Powerful Question

Tonight's Affirmative Statement of TRUTH

*Today I declare
my Divine independence.
I AM free to express my greater yet to be.*

Today's Divine Commentary

ARE YOU ALLOWING YOUR DREAMS TO BE DELAYED?

Never allow laziness and procrastination
to derail or delay your progress
on the road to greatness.

Doing so will create the belief
that there is a lack of time
and cause you to live in a
constant state of "catch up."

DECIDE to live every second of your life
as if you knew that it was your last.
DECLARE that you will not leave this life
without fulfilling your
Divine purpose.

Stop waiting to be, do & have
all of the things that you truly desire.

BE it! DO it! HAVE it!
NOW!!!

Today's Powerful Statement of INTENTION

KNOWING that I AM blessed with the Sacred gift of Divine awareness, Today and everyday I INTENTIONALLY choose only those thoughts, actions & beliefs which shape, influence & support the powerful purpose for my life which is revealed to me everyday by The Most High.

My chief Intention for today is:

_____

_____

_____

_____

_____

_____

_____

_____

_____

_____

_____

_____

Tonight's Classic Inspiration

*Know the true value
of time;
snatch, seize,
and enjoy
every moment of it.
No idleness,
no delay,
no procrastination*
- Lord Chesterfield

Tonight's Affirmative Statement of TRUTH

Today I choose to value every moment and confidently seize every opportunity available to me in order to co-create an amazing life!

Today's Divine Commentary

ARE YOU WILLING TO BE SPIRITUALLY REBORN ?

This human experience is filled with
an ongoing cycle of
Life & Death.

As we master ourselves & learn
the necessary lessons
of each experience,
the old "self" dies so that
a new Self can
be reborn in us.

When we rediscover a sense of Divine
purpose, the discomfort & "mourning"
for our old, lower self will
soon be replaced by
a peace that surpasses all
understanding.

HOLD ON!!
Your Peace is Coming.

Today's Powerful Statement of INTENTION

**KNOWING that I AM blessed with the Sacred gift
of Divine awareness, Today and everyday I
INTENTIONALLY choose only those thoughts,
actions & beliefs which shape, influence & support
the powerful purpose for my life which is revealed
to me everyday by The Most High.**

My chief Intention for today is:

*Therefore if
any man
be in Christ,
he is a
new creature:
old things
are passed away;
behold,
all things
are become new*
-2 Corinthians 5:17

Tonight's Affirmative Statement of TRUTH

*Through the fulfillment of my Divine purpose,
I AM filled with peace as I AM mentally,
spiritually and emotionally
reborn and renewed.*

Today's Divine Commentary

DO YOU HAVE THE COURAGE TO CROSSOVER?

At the border of every perceived
break-down lies the opportunity
for a miraculous
"BREAK-THROUGH."

Too often we pray for relief and release
but hesitate or refuse to take the
necessary steps to cross over
from bondage into
the land of freedom.

One must be courageous enough
to cross the border into
new and foreign land.

We must be willing to enter into
the "wilderness" of Infinite Possibilities
AND TRUST that more good than
we have ever experienced before
will be the welcoming party
that eagerly greets us.

Today's Powerful Statement of INTENTION

KNOWING that I AM blessed with the Sacred gift of Divine awareness, Today and everyday I INTENTIONALLY choose only those thoughts, actions & beliefs which shape, influence & support the powerful purpose for my life which is revealed to me everyday by The Most High.

My chief Intention for today is:

_____

_____

_____

_____

_____

_____

_____

_____

_____

_____

_____

_____

*And I am come down
to deliver them
out of the hand of
the Egyptians,
and to bring them
up out of that land
unto a good land*
- Exodus 3:8

Tonight's Affirmative Statement of TRUTH

Today I trust God as I courageously cross over into the Supreme freedom of my Divine "break-through"

Today's Divine Commentary

WHEN WAS THE LAST TIME YOU EXPRESSED UNIVERSAL LOVE?

Whatever affects one,
affects us all.

We are here for one reason only -
to LOVE on each other
"Soul-Deep" that any appearance
of hurt, pain, loneliness,
poverty or hate
are dissipated and forever
cease to exist.

Simply put, the expression of
Universal Love is the most profound
way of healing the world.

Take this moment right now,
to tell somebody - show somebody
that you love them.

Today's Powerful Statement of INTENTION

KNOWING that I AM blessed with the Sacred gift of Divine awareness, Today and everyday I INTENTIONALLY choose only those thoughts, actions & beliefs which shape, influence & support the powerful purpose for my life which is revealed to me everyday by The Most High.

My chief Intention for today is:

_____

_____

_____

_____

_____

_____

_____

_____

_____

_____

_____

Tonight's Classic Inspiration

*We are
members of
one great body.
Nature planted in us
a mutual love,
and fitted us
for a social life.
We must consider
that we were born
for the good of
the whole*
-Lucius Annaeus Seneca

Tonight's Affirmative Statement of TRUTH

*I AM Divinely connected to ALL Life
and continuously express the Supreme,
healing Love of God to all*

Today's Divine Commentary

WHAT FRUIT WILL THE GARDEN OF YOUR LEGACY BEAR?

Each and every choice that we make is
likened unto a seed planted
in the fertile soil that is
the garden of the future.

The only assurance for the success
of future generations requires,
every day, that you make the sometimes
difficult choice between
living in the shadows and mediocrity
of your fears or BOLDLY
stepping into the Absolute Power
of your inherent Divinity.

What legacy will be left by
the choices you've made today?

Today's Powerful Statement of INTENTION

KNOWING that I AM blessed with the Sacred gift of Divine awareness, Today and everyday I INTENTIONALLY choose only those thoughts, actions & beliefs which shape, influence & support the powerful purpose for my life which is revealed to me everyday by The Most High.

My chief Intention for today is:

Your descendants shall gather your fruits
-Virgil

Tonight's Affirmative Statement of TRUTH

*Today & everyday, I take BOLD responsibility
for the success which will change
many generations to come.*

Today's Divine Commentary

WHAT ARE YOU WILLING TO GIVE UP, TO GO UP?

During the evolutionary awakening
to our Higher Self we must choose
to shed the habitual pattern of
negative thoughts, harmful relationships,
unconsciously created situations
And useless patterns of
drama that keep us stuck
In the "wilderness"
of mediocrity.

In the pursuit of your dreams
What tethers are you willing
to give up in order
to go up?

Today's Powerful Statement of INTENTION

KNOWING that I AM blessed with the Sacred gift of Divine awareness, Today and everyday I INTENTIONALLY choose only those thoughts, actions & beliefs which shape, influence & support the powerful purpose for my life which is revealed to me everyday by The Most High.

My chief Intention for today is:

_____

_____

_____

_____

_____

_____

_____

_____

_____

_____

_____

Tonight's Classic Inspiration

*Fortunate is
the person who
has developed
the self-control
to steer a straight course
toward his objective in life,
without being swayed
from his purpose
by either
commendation
or
condemnation
- Napoleon Hill*

Tonight's Affirmative Statement of TRUTH

Today, in Divine preparation for my purpose,
I free my heart, mind & Spirit.

Today's Divine Commentary

HOW DO YOU HONOR THE SACRED GIFT OF INTUITION?

Intuition is that comforting
"Whisper from with-in"
that tells you that ALL is
as it should be.

Through regular communion with
The Most High and the practice of
mindful meditation we are able to
fine tune our intuition, thereby
eliminating the mental and emotional
burdens of fear, doubt and worry.

Honor your intuition.
For this practice brings about a
conscious state of
"Perfect peace."

Today's Powerful Statement of INTENTION

KNOWING that I AM blessed with the Sacred gift of Divine awareness, Today and everyday I INTENTIONALLY choose only those thoughts, actions & beliefs which shape, influence & support the powerful purpose for my life which is revealed to me everyday by The Most High.

My chief Intention for today is:

_____

_____

_____

_____

_____

_____

_____

_____

_____

_____

_____

*The intuitive mind
is a sacred gift
and the rational mind
is a faithful servant.
We have created
a society
that honors
the servant
and has forgotten
the gift*
-Albert Einstein

Tonight's Affirmative Statement of TRUTH

Today and everyday I AM consciously aware of the influence which I allow to shape my beliefs. I choose to only hold on to beliefs that support the person I AM committed to become.

Today's Divine Commentary

ARE YOU SOULFULLY LIVING YOUR LIFE?

Subscribing to the Soul suffocating rules,
regulations and limiting expectations
of others will often cause us to ignore
the ever present sound of God's voice
calling us to move into
our Greatness.

Never allow another mans limitations to
be placed at the threshold of your dreams.

For no man can see for you
what he fails to see for himself.

We must continually ask
ourSelves this question -
Is this really, truly
AND SOULFULLY
MY life
I'm living?

Today's Powerful Statement of INTENTION

KNOWING that I AM blessed with the Sacred gift of Divine awareness, Today and everyday I INTENTIONALLY choose only those thoughts, actions & beliefs which shape, influence & support the powerful purpose for my life which is revealed to me everyday by The Most High.

My chief Intention for today is:

*You cannot build
character
and
courage
by taking away
man's
initiative
and
independence*
-Abraham Lincoln

Tonight's Affirmative Statement of TRUTH

I AM an expression of the One Power,
One Source, One Love from which
all things flow. I share
this endless supply of Divine love with all.

Today's Divine Commentary

IS THERE ANYTHING THAT GOD CAN NOT DO?

At times we allow ourselves to
falsely believe that our goals,
dreams and visions are
too difficult or impossible
to achieve.

Re-Mind yourself to
continually KNOW,
at a Soul-Deep level,
that EVERYTHING
is possible with God.

And in those moments of doubt
unconscious forgetfulness,
Simply ask yourself,
"If EVERYTHING
is possible with God,
then what does that leave out?

Today's Powerful Statement of INTENTION

KNOWING that I AM blessed with the Sacred gift of Divine awareness, Today and everyday I INTENTIONALLY choose only those thoughts, actions & beliefs which shape, influence & support the powerful purpose for my life which is revealed to me everyday by The Most High.

My chief Intention for today is:

_____

_____

_____

_____

_____

_____

_____

_____

_____

_____

_____

_____

*I can do
all things
through Christ
Which
strengtheneth
me*
-Philippians 4:13

Tonight's Affirmative Statement of TRUTH

*I AM endowed with the same Power
which belongs to the Master Architect
and together we create my Life.*

Today's Divine Commentary

WHAT DIVINE ASSIGNMENT HAVE YOU SAID YES TO?

In order to step into a deeper
understanding of the spiritual
unfolding of this life,
I must Trust
that even in my time of
doubt and uncertainty,
"I AM" now,
and always have been
fully and completely
supported and guided
by God.

TODAY,
I AM boldly saying YES to
ALL of the Divinely ordained
opportunities that are aligning
for me to more fully
express my
True God-Self
to the world.

Today's Powerful Statement of INTENTION

KNOWING that I AM blessed with the Sacred gift of Divine awareness, Today and everyday I INTENTIONALLY choose only those thoughts, actions & beliefs which shape, influence & support the powerful purpose for my life which is revealed to me everyday by The Most High.

My chief Intention for today is:

_____

_____

_____

_____

_____

_____

_____

_____

_____

_____

_____

_____

*Faith is
not being sure
where
you're going
but
going
anyway*
-Fredrick Buechner

Tonight's Affirmative Statement of TRUTH

*Having no doubt that ALL of my steps are
Divinely ordered by the Most High,
I Faithfully place one foot in front of the other
as I walk into my Purpose*

Today's Divine Commentary

IS JUDGMENT HINDERING YOUR SPIRITUAL GROWTH?

So often when we are pointing out
the faults of others it is simply
the "ego's" attempt to resist
the growth necessary to reveal
our own Divine Truth
to the world.

Adopting the practice of going into
Self examination or "Observation mode",
gives us an opportunity to
resolve & dissolve the Self sabotaging
patterns that no longer
serve our Greatest good.

Today Pay attention to yourSelf.

Today's Powerful Statement of INTENTION

KNOWING that I AM blessed with the Sacred gift of Divine awareness, Today and everyday I INTENTIONALLY choose only those thoughts, actions & beliefs which shape, influence & support the powerful purpose for my life which is revealed to me everyday by The Most High.

My chief Intention for today is:

_____

_____

_____

_____

_____

_____

_____

_____

_____

_____

_____

Judge not,
that ye be not judged.
For with what judgment
ye judge,
ye shall be judged:
and with what measure
ye mete,
it shall be measured
to you again
–Matt 7:1-2

Tonight's Affirmative Statement of TRUTH

Seeking to Fully Express
my whole AND Holy God-Self,
I turn within and seek clarity

Today's Divine Commentary

IS YOUR FAITH PLEASING TO GOD?

True Faith never demands details.
Yet so many times our lack of faith
creates a need to know
ALL of the details.

Surely this hinders our ability
to bring forth the manifestation
of our greatest dreams and desires.

The Bible says that without FAITH
it is impossible to please God.

We must trust that beautifully amazing
things will begin to happen
to us and for us when we strengthen
our faith and simply surrender
to that which the Most High
is revealing to the Universe,
through us.

Today's Powerful Statement of INTENTION

KNOWING that I AM blessed with the Sacred gift of Divine awareness, Today and everyday I INTENTIONALLY choose only those thoughts, actions & beliefs which shape, influence & support the powerful purpose for my life which is revealed to me everyday by The Most High.

My chief Intention for today is:

_____

_____

_____

_____

_____

_____

_____

_____

_____

_____

_____

_____

*Faith
is to believe
what we do not see;
the reward
of this faith
is to see
what we believe*
- Saint Augustine

Tonight's Affirmative Statement of TRUTH

*I surrender to the Divine Will
of the Universe and Trust that ALL
that I desire is ALWAYS
unfolding before me & within me*

Today's Divine Commentary

DO YOU RECOGNIZE YOUR GOD-SELF?

The dictionary defines INTUITION as:

1. The act or faculty of
knowing or sensing WITHOUT
the use of rational processes;
IMMEDIATE cognition.

2. Knowledge gained by the
USE of this faculty;
a perceptive insight.

Simply put,
INTUITION is an organic
unfolding of our
not yet revealed,
God-Self;
the Greater Yet to BE;

Today's Powerful Statement of INTENTION

KNOWING that I AM blessed with the Sacred gift of Divine awareness, Today and everyday I INTENTIONALLY choose only those thoughts, actions & beliefs which shape, influence & support the powerful purpose for my life which is revealed to me everyday by The Most High.

My chief Intention for today is:

_____

_____

_____

_____

_____

_____

_____

_____

_____

_____

_____

*He that dwelleth
in the secret place
of The Most High
shall abide
under the shadow
of the Almighty*
- Psalm 91:1

Tonight's Affirmative Statement of TRUTH

*Intuitively I TRUST
the Divine reflection of God
that I AM*

Today's Divine Commentary

HOW ARE YOU USING YOUR DIVINE DOMINION?

Since we are ALL made in the
Image AND Likeness of God,
each and every time you
"tune-in" to your intuition,
the voice that you are hearing
is the Divine voice of God within you,
speaking to you,
through the Super-conscious Mind.

Man & Womb-man have been entrusted
with God-given dominion
over every living thing that
moves upon the earth.

RESPECT & TRUST
the God in you to
guide and inform
your EVERY decision
on this journey called life.

KNOWING that I AM blessed with the Sacred gift of Divine awareness, Today and everyday I INTENTIONALLY choose only those thoughts, actions & beliefs which shape, influence & support the powerful purpose for my life which is revealed to me everyday by The Most High.

My chief Intention for today is:

*And God
created man
in his own image,
in the image of God
created he him;
male and female
created he
them*
-Genesis 1:27

Tonight's Affirmative Statement of TRUTH

Today I consciously connect
to the guidance of
Supreme Consciousness

Today's Divine Commentary

DO YOU KNOW THAT YOU HAVE WINGS?

Despair and depression are often the
monsters that dwell in
the experience we call
"the dark night of the soul."

Who knew that the long darkness
that once brought fear and uncertainty
to the cocooned caterpillar would soon
begin an unfolding of
beautifully colorful wings
with which the butterfly would soar
to new heights? Revealing a view of life
which has always been readily available
- just on the other side
of darkness.

You too, have beautiful wings!
Use them to soar into
the next beautiful phase
of your life

Today's Powerful Statement of INTENTION

KNOWING that I AM blessed with the Sacred gift of Divine awareness, Today and everyday I INTENTIONALLY choose only those thoughts, actions & beliefs which shape, influence & support the powerful purpose for my life which is revealed to me everyday by The Most High.

My chief Intention for today is:

*Once you stop clinging
and let things be,
you'll be free,
even of birth and death.
You'll transform
everything*
-Bodhidharma

Tonight's Affirmative Statement of TRUTH

Joyously I spread my wings
as I step into the Radiant
Light of Gods unfolding Beauty

Today's Divine Commentary

ARE YOU TUNED IN TO THE VOICE OF GOD?

The supernatural emanation of
Divine Mind continually,
ALWAYS without ceasing,
communicates its instruction
with concise clarity.

In order to be in alignment
with your true calling,
you must set aside SACRED time
EVERY day
to intentionally tune
Your intuition to the frequency
of God's voice.

Once you have received the message
which is specifically intended for you,
be sure that the actions that you take
line up with the instruction
you have been given.

Today's Powerful Statement of INTENTION

KNOWING that I AM blessed with the Sacred gift of Divine awareness, Today and everyday I INTENTIONALLY choose only those thoughts, actions & beliefs which shape, influence & support the powerful purpose for my life which is revealed to me everyday by The Most High.

My chief Intention for today is:

_____

_____

_____

_____

_____

_____

_____

_____

_____

_____

_____

_____

*When deeds
and words
are in accord,
the whole world
is transformed*
- *Chuang Tzu*

Tonight's Affirmative Statement of TRUTH

*Knowing that my steps are Divinely ordered
by the Most High, I confidently move forward
on my purpose-filled journey*

DO YOU KNOW
THAT IT'S NOT
ABOUT YOU?

The ego or that less evolved part
of the human personality
has a way of creating an illusion
that the spiritual work that we do is
to be done so that we can be elevated
onto the public pedestal in order to get
the praise and adoration of man.

WRONG!

This perspective creates a
duality which suggests a separation
between us and our God-Self.

When we understand and accept that
WE are the Divine vessels through which
The Most High works all Miracles,
the illusion of separation will cease
to exist and we will begin to exhibit a deeply
spiritual and unshakable confidence in
our work, our purpose & our mission.

Today's Powerful Statement of INTENTION

KNOWING that I AM blessed with the Sacred gift of Divine awareness, Today and everyday I INTENTIONALLY choose only those thoughts, actions & beliefs which shape, influence & support the powerful purpose for my life which is revealed to me everyday by The Most High.

My chief Intention for today is:

_____

_____

_____

_____

_____

_____

_____

_____

_____

_____

_____

*I
and
the Father
are
one*
- *John 10:30*

Tonight's Affirmative Statement of TRUTH

Knowing that my work is Gods work.
I eagerly surrender
This vessel to the Universal service of ALL

Today's Divine Commentary

AM I WILLING TO BE MY BROTHER'S KEEPER?

In today's fragile social,
economic and emotional environments,
we never know where,
on the "cliff"
someone may be standing.

We have the power to
either push them
over the edge or
pull them in,
wrap our arms around them
and let them know
that although
it may not look like it right now....
"this too shall pass!"

Today's Powerful Statement of INTENTION

KNOWING that I AM blessed with the Sacred gift of Divine awareness, Today and everyday I INTENTIONALLY choose only those thoughts, actions & beliefs which shape, influence & support the powerful purpose for my life which is revealed to me everyday by The Most High.

My chief Intention for today is:

*How far you go in life
depends on your
being tender
with the young,
Compassionate
with the aged,
sympathetic
with the striving
and tolerant
of the weak and strong.
Because someday
in life you will have been
all of these*
- George Washington Carver

Tonight's Affirmative Statement of TRUTH

I AM LOVE,
and I share this endless supply
of Divine love with all.

Today's Divine Commentary

ARE YOU LIVING YOUR LIFE FULL OUT?

What if
your TRUTH challenged
everything that everyone else
thought of you.

What if it required
that you do the opposite
of what everyone else
expected of you?

Many of us meander through life
under the constant control and censorship
of what we believe others will approve of
or accept for us.

Too often we never allow ourselves to
explore the depths of our TRUE
desires in life.

This gift called life is too precious
to not be lived
FULL OUT.

Today's Powerful Statement of INTENTION

KNOWING that I AM blessed with the Sacred gift of Divine awareness, Today and everyday I INTENTIONALLY choose only those thoughts, actions & beliefs which shape, influence & support the powerful purpose for my life which is revealed to me everyday by The Most High.

My chief Intention for today is:

_____

_____

_____

_____

_____

_____

_____

_____

_____

_____

_____

Give
every man
thine ear,
but few
thy voice
- William Shakespeare

Tonight's Affirmative Statement of TRUTH

Unconcerned with what others will think,
Today I CHOOSE
to live my life to the FULLEST

Today's Divine Commentary

IS FEAR STANDING IN THE WAY OF YOUR JOY?

How often do you dutifully stand guard,
blocking the doorway of opportunity
which most assuredly leads to
the very success you've prayed for
in your future,
because of the lingering stench of
a perceived failure
from your past?

Take heed that ALL of
the love, success & wealth
that you TRULY desire
at the core of your being;
the peace that you pray for every night,
when no one but you and God are listening,
waits for you
right on the other side
of your pain, doubt, worry and fear.

Today's Powerful Statement of INTENTION

KNOWING that I AM blessed with the Sacred gift of Divine awareness, Today and everyday I INTENTIONALLY choose only those thoughts, actions & beliefs which shape, influence & support the powerful purpose for my life which is revealed to me everyday by The Most High.

My chief Intention for today is:

_____

_____

_____

_____

_____

_____

_____

_____

_____

_____

_____

*Fear is
the most
devastating
of all
human emotions.
Man has no trouble
like the paralyzing
effects of fear*
- Paul Parker

Tonight's Affirmative Statement of TRUTH

Today I RELEASE
everything that stands in the way of my Joy;
beginning with fear

Today's Divine Commentary

WHAT MIRACLES WILL YOU PERFORM TODAY?

The earthquakes in our lives show up
as the necessary catalyst to
shake us out of the unconscious,
dis-empowering state of mediocrity
that we call "normal."

Do not squander the untapped gift
of potentiality which life eagerly
offers up to you
each and every day.

We are Divinely created to
be powerful co-creators of
EVERYday miracles.

Today's Powerful Statement of INTENTION

KNOWING that I AM blessed with the Sacred gift of Divine awareness, Today and everyday I INTENTIONALLY choose only those thoughts, actions & beliefs which shape, influence & support the powerful purpose for my life which is revealed to me everyday by The Most High.

My chief Intention for today is:

_____

_____

_____

_____

_____

_____

_____

_____

_____

_____

_____

Tonight's Classic Inspiration

*There are powers
inside of you which,
if you could
discover and use,
would make of you
everything
you ever dreamed
or imagined
you could become*
- Orison Swett Marden

Tonight's Affirmative Statement of TRUTH

I UNLEASH
my indwelling POWER
and EVERYDAY
I create Miracles

Today's Divine Commentary

3 SPIRITUAL STEPS TO CO-CREATION

1) See it.
Have a clear & detailed vision
of exactly what u desire
AND why

2) Speak it.
In the Holy scriptures,
The Law of Command
was plainly displayed by God
during the creation story.
Preceding the manifestation of
ANYTHING we see the words,
And God said,
"Let there be..."

3) Sow it.
If u desire growth and Prosperity
you must Roll up your sleeves
and plant the seeds.
DO YOUR PART!

Today's Powerful Statement of INTENTION

KNOWING that I AM blessed with the Sacred gift of Divine awareness, Today and everyday I INTENTIONALLY choose only those thoughts, actions & beliefs which shape, influence & support the powerful purpose for my life which is revealed to me everyday by The Most High.

My chief Intention for today is:

*There is
no greater joy
than that of
Feeling oneself
a creator.
The triumph of life
is expressed by
creation*
- Henri Bergson

Tonight's Affirmative Statement of TRUTH

By aligning my thoughts, words AND actions,
today I DO my part
to co-Create the life I desire

Today's Divine Commentary

WHAT LIMITATIONS HAVE YOU PLACED ON GOD?

What If EVERYTHING
you ever prayed for-
a Loving Soul-mate, Unlimited Wealth
or that deeply profound
Life changing experience-
ALL showed up wrapped
in sandpaper?

Would you recognize it as
"The Answer to your Prayers?"

In other words, what if
your greatest blessing
shows up in a way that is
completely unconventional or opposite
of your current expectation?

Remove the blinding limitations
from your mind and see the
true Glory of God.

Today's Powerful Statement of INTENTION

KNOWING that I AM blessed with the Sacred gift of Divine awareness, Today and everyday I INTENTIONALLY choose only those thoughts, actions & beliefs which shape, influence & support the powerful purpose for my life which is revealed to me everyday by The Most High.

My chief Intention for today is:

_____

_____

_____

_____

_____

_____

_____

_____

_____

_____

_____

_____

*God is
a circle
whose center
is everywhere
and
circumference
nowhere*
- Voltaire

Tonight's Affirmative Statement of TRUTH

I PRAY
for the Opening of my Spiritual Eyes
that I may RE-cognize the God in ALL

Today's Divine Commentary

WHERE HAVE YOU PLACED YOUR FAITH?

In the midst of difficulties,
when we are unable to see the reason,
understand the outcome or
make peace with our circumstances,
we often find ourselves asking the questions,
"What is my purpose?"
or "Why am I here?"

In those moments we must
have Faith and KNOW
that there is a Divine reason
for EVERY moment
of our existence.

We MUST KEEP ON BELIEVING
in our dreams, our purpose
AND our calling.

For The Most High
has beautiful intentions to bless us
so that the world can be blessed
through the fulfillment of our destiny.

Today's Powerful Statement of INTENTION

KNOWING that I AM blessed with the Sacred gift of Divine awareness, Today and everyday I INTENTIONALLY choose only those thoughts, actions & beliefs which shape, influence & support the powerful purpose for my life which is revealed to me everyday by The Most High.

My chief Intention for today is:

_____

_____

_____

_____

_____

_____

_____

_____

_____

_____

_____

_____

*Faith is
the daring
of the soul to
go farther
than it can see*
-William Newton Clark

Tonight's Affirmative Statement of TRUTH

Today I BOLDLY and Faithfully SEEK
the fulfillment of my Divine Destiny

Today's Divine Commentary

KNOW YE NOT THAT YE ARE THE LIGHT OF THE WORLD?

Regardless of race,
status, education,
finances or bloodline,
there is a beautiful & DIVINE Light
that illuminates the Soul
of EVERY man, woman,
boy & girl
on the planet.

CHOOSE to INTENTIONALLY
Shine your Light
in ALL dark places,
for only the Light of Love,
Compassion, Forgiveness,
and Patience can heal
the wounds of this world.

NEVER fear
the LIGHT
that IS YOU!!

Today's Powerful Statement of INTENTION

KNOWING that I AM blessed with the Sacred gift of Divine awareness, Today and everyday I INTENTIONALLY choose only those thoughts, actions & beliefs which shape, influence & support the powerful purpose for my life which is revealed to me everyday by The Most High.

My chief Intention for today is:

_____

_____

_____

_____

_____

_____

_____

_____

_____

_____

_____

Tonight's Classic Inspiration

*Ye are the light
of the world.
A city that is set
on a hill cannot be hid...
Let your light so shine
before men,
that they may see
your good works,
and glorify your Father
which is in heaven*
- Matt5:14-16

Tonight's Affirmative Statement of TRUTH

Boldly!! Brilliantly!! Brightly!!
I SHINE!!

Today's Divine Commentary

ARE YOU SHOWING THE WORLD YOUR TRUE BEAUTY?

In the hustle and bustle of life
we often neglect ourselves by
Taking on habits that take a toll
on our outer appearance.

This body that we have been given
is simply the outer shell (vessel)
which "houses" the Divine Spirit
which dwells within.

In other words,
our bodies are our visual
RE-presentation to the world
of the God within.

Today, I encourage you to take time,
make time to pamper and
take care of your body.

Make sure that the outside is
a "Divinely Delicious" reflection
of your Inner Beauty.

Today's Powerful Statement of INTENTION

KNOWING that I AM blessed with the Sacred gift of Divine awareness, Today and everyday I INTENTIONALLY choose only those thoughts, actions & beliefs which shape, influence & support the powerful purpose for my life which is revealed to me everyday by The Most High.

My chief Intention for today is:

Tonight's Classic Inspiration

*Though we travel
the world over
to find the beautiful,
we must carry it
with us
or we find it not*
- *Ralph Waldo Emerson*

Tonight's Affirmative Statement of TRUTH

Knowing that the "me" that you see is a "Divinely Delicious" reflection of the God Within, I pamper, love & take care of my body temple

Today's Divine Commentary

ARE YOU PREPARED TO RECEIVE YOUR BLESSING?

Quite often on the road to success
we look to avoid the hard work
and preparation
which takes place in that space
between here and "there",
otherwise known as
"the process."

Too often, we seek the "short cut"
to a destination (place of Destiny)
for which we are not yet prepared.

I just LOVE how the Universe ALWAYS
sends us EXACTLY what we need at
the EXACT time that we are
ready, willing & able
to receive it.

Only through proper preparation can we
be blessed; therefore, keep your eyes,
heart & hands WIDE OPEN
'cause If you STAY ready
you don't have to GET ready.

Today's Powerful Statement of INTENTION

KNOWING that I AM blessed with the Sacred gift of Divine awareness, Today and everyday I INTENTIONALLY choose only those thoughts, actions & beliefs which shape, influence & support the powerful purpose for my life which is revealed to me everyday by The Most High.

My chief Intention for today is:

_____

_____

_____

_____

_____

_____

_____

_____

_____

_____

_____

Tonight's Classic Inspiration

*I will
prepare
and someday
my chance
will come.*
-Abraham Lincoln

Tonight's Affirmative Statement of TRUTH

*I AM Whole Soul surrendered
to the process and fully ready to
receive my Blessing*

Today's Divine Commentary

HOW MANY WAYS ARE YOU LOVED?

In this moment I AM
tearfully overjoyed for
the Magnificently omniscient
ways in which
I AM Loved & Supported
by God.

There has never been a day
where the Sun has not risen
to provide warmth & Light.

Never a moment
when my heart failed to beat
to the Divine rhythm
of the Universe.

Never a time
when my blood did not
Miraculously flow against gravity
in order to sustain my body.

Thank you Father/Mother God!!!!

Today's Powerful Statement of INTENTION

KNOWING that I AM blessed with the Sacred gift of Divine awareness, Today and everyday I INTENTIONALLY choose only those thoughts, actions & beliefs which shape, influence & support the powerful purpose for my life which is revealed to me everyday by The Most High.

My chief Intention for today is:

*Therefore
I say unto you,
be not anxious
for your life,
what ye shall eat,
or what ye shall drink;
nor yet for your body,
what ye shall put on.
Is not the life
more than the food,
and the body
than the raiment?*
- Matt 6:25

Tonight's Affirmative Statement of TRUTH

EVERY moment of EVERY day,
I AM Loved with a Supreme Love

One Powerful Question